Charting Our Course

Charting Our Course

Renewing the Church's Teaching Ministry

Linda R. Isham

Judson Press ® Valley Forge

Charting Our Course: Renewing the Church's Teaching Ministry
© 1997 Judson Press, Valley Forge, PA 19482-0851

Bible quotations in this volume are from the New Revised Standard Version of the Bible, copyright © 1989 by the Division of Christian Education of the National Council of the Churches of Christ in the United States of America. Used by permission. All rights reserved.

Library of Congress Cataloging-in-Publication Data
Isham, Linda R.
  Charting our course : renewing the church's teaching ministry / Linda R. Isham.
    p. cm.
  Includes bibliographical references.
  ISBN 0-8170-1254-0 (pbk. : alk. paper)
  1. Christian education. 2. Christian education—Study and teaching. I. Title.
BV1464.I74 1997
268—dc21   96-39452

Printed in the U.S.A.

05 04 03 02 01 00 99 98

10 9 8 7 6 5 4 3 2

To my first teachers, my parents,
Webb and Ardilla Isham

Contents

Foreword

Linda Isham's fine new book is a needed, accessible, and practical contribution to the literature of Christian education. It is needed because it takes seriously the times in which we live, which she describes—rightly, to my mind—as a wilderness time, a time of searching for new maps. It is accessible because it uses the language of that search with great care and addresses the reader without condescension or artifice. It is practical because it offers specific and detailed instruction in how to create a renewed teaching ministry.

The book is also rich in themes around which the ideas and the practices cluster, and readers will undoubtedly be moved by many of them as they choose for their own teaching ministries the ones that have the most currency in their church, family, and work situations. Nevertheless, I suspect that the following key words will be particularly important to educational work because they resound so clearly for our own times. These are the master themes of search, Scripture, community, and experience.

Search is a dominant and recurring theme, carried throughout the book and described variously as looking for new maps while working with old ones, trying new paths, and recognizing destinations as we encounter them. The search is aided by many suggestions for pilgrims in the educational wilderness, especially and notably the excellent directions on how to clarify mission and vision and how to distinguish between adaptive and foundational change.

The search is also accompanied by a beautiful and poetic familiarity with *Scripture*. The chapter on destinations, for example, gives the instruction, "When you cross over the Jordan into the land of Canaan, . . . you shall take possession of the land and settle in it, for I have given you the land to possess" (Numbers 33:51b,53). The chapter on striking out and trying new paths is grounded in the counsel of Deuteronomy (2:2-3) to "head north" because as a people the wanderers had been skirting the hill country long enough and it was now time to take action. But Scripture is also used as a criterion for educators: the biblical story remains central throughout, no matter what instructions the author is offering.

Community is a third major theme. An entire chapter underscores this under the rubric of "journeying not alone." But each chapter also underscores community as does each set of questions Isham offers (and she provides many of these). For example, in chapter 3, she is very specific in asking readers to reflect on how the changes they are proposing—whether adaptive or foundational changes—have an impact on community even as they build it. She also probes how such changes communicate who God is for this community, asking the community to engage in such probes along with her. She reminds the reader that if any of us teach in isolation from the rest of the faith community, we not only miss opportunities, but we also propagate individualistic faith. In other words, for this author, and in this book, Christianity is a communal faith.

And finally, there is *experience*. The author's experience informs the book throughout each page, and she draws on this experience confidently. Obviously, she has "been there" and is there still. But she also uses teaching ministries and experiences suggested by others. She refers to writers (there is a strong appendix with many resources), pastors, faithful teachers, and leaders from the past. She cites those who have developed ministry teams rather than traditional committees, the practice of prayer partners, and "Sabbath" Sundays— even as she urges readers to trust their own experience and to draw on their own insights in mapping the way toward renewing the teaching ministry of the church.

—Maria Harris
Author of *Proclaim Jubilee!* and *Jubilee Time*

Preface

As I began writing this book, I realized that it had been in process in my mind for some time, parts of it for thirty years. The impetus to put something down in print came in January 1996 following a conference in which Maria Harris guided a group of us in thinking about the biblical jubilee and its meaning for Christian education today. So at the outset I am grateful to Maria (for agreeing to write the foreword also) and my colleagues who interacted with her on that topic. Bits and pieces related to those conversations appear in the following chapters.

The basic thesis of this book is that we in the church are in a wilderness time concerning the teaching ministry. (Some would say that all of the church's ministries are in such a wilderness time.) The old maps that have told us how to do Christian education are out of date, and the new ones aren't yet available. We don't, however, have to sit and do nothing. We can be mapping the way into the future of the church's teaching ministry. Critical to our mapping is regaining our sense of God's purpose for these ministries and having a vision for the future. This book does not have *the* solution; rather it suggests some things that can be done in such an in-between time. They may serve us well in the future, too. There is a combination of theory and practice throughout the book. My list-making tendency emerges in several places with lists of things to think about and/or do. In order to fully record your responses to the questions in the sections called "Reflect and act on the following," you may find it helpful to keep a notebook handy. There are appendices at the end, and appendices B, C, and E may be copied for use in local church congregations.

Most of all I want these words to be words of encouragement. Many teachers and Christian education leaders I meet are discouraged. They seek words of support. I hope the pages that follow are just the encouraging words they need.

This book wouldn't have been possible without the help of many people including my friend and former colleague Bud Carroll; colleagues Jean Kim and Don Ng from Educational Ministries of the American Baptist Churches in the U.S.A.; several local church educators who encouraged me (including Verity Jones, Debbie Gravell, and Soozi Ford); Jean and Brendon Bass, pastors of West Parish Congregational Church in Bethel, Maine, who loaned me space (and a place to plug in my laptop) where I could write while on vacation; family members who put up with my frequent conversation about the book; Marcia Jessen, who helped in checking details and preparing the manuscript for submission; and Hal Rast and Kristy Pullen of Judson Press, who said yes when I first proposed the book. And alongside these persons whom I've named are countless others who have nurtured and challenged me and have been my partners in the church's teaching ministry. I'm grateful to all of them.

Chapter 1

Looking for New Maps While Working with Old Ones

If only we had died by the hand of the LORD in the land of Egypt, when we sat by the fleshpots and ate our fill of bread; for you have brought us out into this wilderness. . . .

—Exodus 16:3

Some of us remember the good old days when the church's teaching-ministry maps were clear and accurate. The primary vehicle for the church's teaching ministry was the Sunday church school. People readily enrolled and attended. There were closely graded classes, especially for children and youth. All the spots on the teaching staff were filled. Teachers taught for an entire year and attended regular training events and/or workers' conferences. Team teaching meant a team of people who planned and taught together every Sunday during the year. Parents came, brought their children, and stayed themselves for an adult class.

The last thirty years or so have seen a steady decline in the enrollment and attendance figures for Sunday church school in many denominations. Children come on their own or are dropped off by parents who don't stay. Youth sports teams practice and play on Sunday mornings. Children of divorce may attend one or two Sundays a month. Teachers are more difficult to recruit and often don't want to go to teacher-training events. Many people within and without the church are biblically illiterate. Many seek meaning for their lives yet seem reluctant to join a congregation and commit themselves to ongoing learning.

Many of us ask questions such as: What's wrong today? What are we doing wrong? and Why, when we work so hard, aren't there results? We sometimes hear complaints such as: We used to have a large Sunday church school, but now look at it. Why can't we do it like we used to? Teachers surely aren't committed like they used to be. Sometimes we go on to ask, Why isn't it working today? What is working? Who has some answers? What other teaching/learning models might we explore?

The time is akin to wandering in the wilderness. Some students of the church say we are in between paradigms (*Webster's New Collegiate Dictionary* defines paradigm as "an outstandingly clear pattern"). The old ways don't seem to be working or, at least, working as well. We've seen few if any maps for the future. We've lost our sense of direction. The future is unclear and uncertain, and we hear complaints, not unlike those of the Israelites wandering in the wilderness and complaining to Moses and Aaron (Exodus 16ff). We seek new charts and maps and paths.

Finding Our Way

When you look at a road map, usually you see more than one way to get where you want to go. You have a choice of interstate highways or back roads or city streets. If you're traveling with someone, you consult with them about what the best way might be, especially if they've traveled the way before or have a good sense of direction. And if you get lost, you might even stop and ask directions. Sometimes you discover broken lines on the map indicating the road has not been completed yet; it's under construction.

That's the kind of place we find ourselves in regarding the church's teaching ministry today. The finished highway has ended, and the journey now is taking place on a road that's under construction. In some sense we're in uncharted territory. I'm reminded of the times when backpacking that I would lose the trail marked with blazes. I would sometimes find myself going ahead and then backtracking or trying one path and then another rather tentatively. Since I never backpacked alone, there were always other people to suggest a direction to take, check a map, share in being lost, and encourage one another. Sometimes we stopped and rested and got our bearings. Together we would take some risks. There was always a solution among us and celebratory ice cream cones at the end of the trip.

The journey didn't stop for the Israelites when they reached the wilderness. It continued—to be sure not always as they wished or without complaint—and for forty years! Our journey in today's teaching ministry continues as well. We can put this "wilderness" time to good use. We also can view it as a time for remembering, for celebrating, for learning, for acting in hope for the future. It's a time that needs to be characterized by six kinds of action: conversation, experimentation, study, sabbath, grieving and release, and thanksgiving. These steps don't need to take place in a certain order, but maintaining some kind of rhythm between them would seem to be useful. Most of them can take place simultaneously. Let's take a look now at each of these actions.

Conversation

This is a time to be talking about all sorts of ideas, questions, and ponderings with all sorts of people. It's a time for informal discussion, dialogue, and visiting, as well as for more intentional, deliberative discussion or consultation. The informal discussions don't require coming to conclusions or making decisions or taking actions; the intentional discussions may. And one of the good things about informal conversation is that it isn't dependent upon taking time to plan it or getting it on everyone's calendar. You can start one as soon as you close this book and find another person or pick up the phone or get on the Internet to talk with someone. Conversation is a readily available tool for each of us.

Some recent experiences of mine made me see the potential value of conversation in finding our way in the church's teaching ministry. One was an unplanned conversation, and two were intentionally planned conversations—one labeled just that. The impromptu conversation happened on a plane as I was returning from a gathering of national and regional Christian education leaders. The plane wasn't crowded, and part way through the flight a regional colleague came and asked if he could sit and talk a bit about some things he was thinking about and working on. It was a lively and energizing conversation. We each had a chance to spin out some ideas about different ways to be doing the church's ministry. We asked questions, shared back-burner ideas, and mentioned resources to each other. And the conversation has continued in a couple of phone calls and a FAX.

One of the planned conversations took place among three people who responded to an invitation to talk about young-adult ministry and how a region might assist churches in this arena. The three people discussed what they were doing, what they were seeking, what had and hadn't worked, how future conversations might take place, and how a team of interested persons might be available to churches wanting to explore ministry with young adults. The second planned conversation took place among a small group of local church educators gathered to share Lenten resources and discuss competencies most needed by local church educators. That conversation took place over lunch and included some important personal sharing.

Conversations need to take place about what is working, what isn't working, why teaching is important to the Christian community, what the purpose of teaching is, how best to do it today and in the future, and about our failures, successes, and hopes. We might describe such conversation groups as encouragement groups. What's needed in this wilderness time are attentive listening to one another's fears, longings, and hopes; a nonjudgmental place to risk sharing even the most far-fetched idea or previously unasked question; and mutual encouragement.

Let's be reminded and remind each other of the words of encouragement found in 2 Thessalonians 2:16-17: "May our Lord Jesus Christ himself and God our Father, who loved us and through grace gave us eternal comfort and good hope, comfort your hearts and strengthen them in every good work and word."

Reflect and act on the following:

1. What two or three challenges are being faced in the teaching ministry of your congregation?

2. What are your hopes for the teaching ministry of your congregation?

3. What are the one or two greatest disappointments about the teaching ministry of your congregation?

4. Which of the above would you most like to talk about with someone?

(If you are doing this exercise as a group, stop and discuss these questions now. If you are doing this exercise alone, move ahead to questions 5 and 6.)

5. What two persons would you most like to talk with about these things?

6. How soon can you arrange such a conversation?

Experimentation

Loren B. Mead, in *The Once and Future Church: Reinventing the Congregation for a New Mission Frontier*, writes about the principle of working experimentally: "In a time of change, when pressure and opportunity for change are not the same everywhere, we badly need innovators, people and groups who will take a stab at a new way with the freedom to fail."[1] While Mead primarily seems to be addressing judicatory or regional denominational leaders, he offers some requirements for such experimentation that can be helpful for local church leaders.

While we no longer can plan for permanence and uniformity, we need to make commitments that are sufficiently long. The length of time needed for an experiment depends on the size and scope of the given experiment. Knowing that we're trying something for a limited period of time can free us to risk things we might not if we were thinking at the outset that the change was permanent. Consistency in leadership for an experimental program or project is helpful, if at all possible. Although changes in leadership can undercut experimental projects, broad-based ownership can help projects weather a leadership-change storm.

Critical to any experimental program or project is capturing and communicating learnings. Planning for this from the beginning assures that it will happen. During an experiment and at its conclusion ask: What happened? What worked? What didn't? and Why? What could be improved, added, or deleted? If we were to do it again, what would we do differently? Keeping others informed of what's happening and how the project is progressing is important throughout the process as well as at its conclusion. Setting up a regular time and place for such communication will help people look for and expect it.

I remember a group conversation one fall in which a man from one church shared an idea for a program he wanted to begin. Though he was somewhat hesitant, he described his dream of a night out for parents when children would be cared for at the church. A woman from another church suggested he try it weekly during the Christmas shopping season between Thanksgiving and Christmas—a length of time suitable for such a program.

Recently I met with three congregations who were exploring the possibility of a joint Sunday church school. All three churches have small Sunday church schools, and they are located in close proximity to each other. Two of the churches had conducted joint summer worship services and were especially ready to explore a joint church school. They showed a readiness to try a new thing and a willingness to explore some of the challenges presented. One church decided not to continue the conversation after checking it out with the congregation. After further conversation, the two remaining churches decided that they would not have the involvement of the minimum number of participants needed to adequately sustain a joint Sunday church school (and it would require considerable work). They did decide to collaborate on some joint children's programming during the summer.

Reflect and act on the following:

1. What program idea have you been wanting to try?

2. What would you hope to learn by trying it?

(If you are doing this exercise as a group, stop and discuss these questions now. If you are doing this exercise alone, continue with question 3.)

3. How might you try the program idea, and with whom would you do so?

Study

The study action is twofold: studying the biblical story and studying our world. One without the other is incomplete. Both are necessary on this wilderness journey. But I suspect we need to come to both of them with a learning stance that I like to call "as though for the first time." The phrase isn't new with me. I'm indebted for it to Patricia W. Van Ness.[2]

The Biblical Story

In our study of the biblical story I think we need to turn particularly to stories that can help us understand how teaching was done in Old Testament times and in New Testament times. Later I'll suggest some stories for study, but first let me propose some approaches to this Bible study. This is not an academic pursuit. We pursue this study of the Bible because we want to know more about what the Bible says about teaching the faith, to grow in our own faith, and to gain a vision for what we must be doing today to make a difference. Our goal is the transformation of ourselves and the teaching ministry of the church. Indeed, there is much to learn about this teaching ministry from the Bible.

I believe the community is called to this study. It won't work if everyone is doing it individually, and it won't work if only the members of the board of Christian education engage in it. It needs to be a broadly based church effort that's intergenerational in scope.

Components of the Bible study include reading the story (perhaps memorizing it), looking at the setting and social situation, identifying with the people in the story, and applying the story to our own lives and ministries. Passages for the study are Exodus 12:21–15:21; Mark 9:33-37; Luke 10:25-37; and Acts 2:1-42 (or the following verses: 1-7, 14-15, 22-24, and 36-42). Here are suggested steps for studying these stories:

1. Begin by reading the Bible story from several different translations or from a translation not often used by the group.

2. Continue by researching the setting and social situation of the story. One or two persons might do this for the group. Here's where commentaries, Bible dictionaries, and atlases can be helpful, especially when the information from them is presented in interesting ways.

3. Empathize with the characters in the story by having each group member identify with one specific character as the story is read and afterward share feelings experienced through hearing the story. Invite group members to recount similar experiences in their own lives.

4. Conclude the study by providing a variety of ways for group members to identify applications they can make in their own lives or actions the congregation can take. Music, drama, art activities, discussion, and writing are all methods to use in the application phase of Bible study.

Our World

In our study of the world we can make use of our daily

learnings from reading newspapers (including the cartoons), viewing television, listening to the radio, being on the Internet, being involved in a variety of community activities, as well as from our experiences at school, in the workplace, and at home. Though each of us has different experiences and will see the world through our own lens, we will find we hold many things in common and may share some of the same concerns about the society of which we are a part. It will be important not to limit ourselves just to what we already know. The intent is to expand what we know about the world—to enlarge our world-view—to see what the implications are for the church and its teaching ministry today. We can bring these life experiences to our study of the Bible, thereby bringing the Bible and life together.

One way to approach the study of our world is to use stories, as was suggested for Bible study. We can share stories from our own experience or from reading, listening, or viewing. Following our sharing we might identify things about which we want to know more and assign further research to group members. We can use a variety of methods for the sharing of and/or reporting on the research—from debate to interview to panel discussion to video.

There are a variety of topics we'll want to explore, such as computer technology, year-round schooling, the impact of television, multicultural education, divorce, single-parent families, violence and crime, religious pluralism, roles of men and women, abuse and neglect of children, race relations, materialism, and at-risk factors for youth. You'll want to look at your community and situation and make your own list of study areas.

Reflect and act on the following:

1. Make a list of areas of concern about your community and the world that you feel your church should study.

2. Read over the list and choose the three most important to study now.

3. Make a list of the resources available to help you study each of the three areas. These could include people, organizations, books, videos, and so forth.

(If you are doing this exercise alone, stop now, before moving to step 4, and plan how you will share your thinking with others and invite their ideas.)

4. Make the necessary plans to get started in studying one of the areas.

Sabbath

Elizabeth Yates in *A Book of Hours* tells of the American Indian guide who was leading a group through high mountain country:

> Before leaving the campsite, he walked away to stand silently beside a tree. His gaze was directed ahead to the trail they would all soon be following. Some sections of it he could see, but when it dipped into the valley, crossed a stream and went up a distant slope he could follow it only in anticipation. In silence he prepared himself for what was visible and for what was unseen. When he felt ready, he signalled to the group to follow him.[3]

I've found that description of a *sabbath* moment helpful more than once over the years. It's an old, old concept found several places in the biblical record. The sabbath theme is woven throughout the biblical story. The concept appears in Genesis 2:2-3. The verb *rested* (Hebrew *shabat*) found in those verses is the basis of the noun *sabbath*.[4] We see the sabbath theme appearing again in Exodus 16:22-30 and

31:12-17. It is part of the jubilee tradition as well (Leviticus 25 and Isaiah 61). Jesus practiced sabbath by going to the synagogue (Luke 4:16) or going apart from his disciples and praying (Luke 6:12). We, too, are commanded to observe sabbath, with suggestions about the frequency such as the seventh day and the seventh year.

Sabbath is desperately needed at this point in the teaching-ministry journey, and we need not wait until the seventh day or the seventh year. We can take sabbath moments individually, at the start and/or close of meetings and classes and at many other times and in many other ways that you will think of. The biblical sabbath suggests that we do several things: rest from our normal activities or busyness, get quiet, pray, and worship. Sabbath needs to become an integral part of who we are as a community on a journey. We need to become known again as a sabbath people. But it won't happen without practice. So I invite you to practice sabbath using one of the following suggestions or some from your own storehouse of ideas. Prepare for what is visible to you and for what is unknown in your teaching ministry.

Some Sabbath Practice Suggestions

• Spend a few moments in silence at the start of each day, listening for and to God's voice, and gradually increase the length of time spent in silence.

• Observe two minutes of silence at the beginning of at least one meal a day.

• Begin each of your board or committee meetings with a brief period of silence followed by prayer.

• Choose a sabbath partner. Together support each other in spending moments in silence on some regular basis to which you've agreed.

• Set aside some time every seventh day for a period of silence and prayer.

• Begin your times of silence by repeating the words of Isaiah 40:31:

> . . . those who wait for the LORD
>   shall renew their strength,
> they shall mount up with wings
>   like eagles,
> they shall run and not be weary,
>   they shall walk and not faint.

Grieving and Release

I sometimes feel that we carry around great burdens of guilt and disappointment or anger for the way things are or aren't in the church's teaching ministry today and that often we are either unwilling or afraid to express those feelings. Those of us who have been around for awhile have deep and long memories of the way it used to be. We may continue to hold old and sometimes unrealistic expectations. At the same time folks newer to the Christian education scene may feel that they've not been allowed a fair chance to try out some new ideas.

It's hard to let go of memories. We sometimes dump those feelings and expectations on others. I can remember what it felt like when I was a director of Christian education in a local church in the 1960s and one of the dear saints of the church frequently reminded me that the Sunday school used to number three hundred members. I always felt she was implying that I was not doing my job because it no longer was that large. And we both ended up carrying burdens.

Recently I've been part of groups in which corporately we have owned up to some of our disappointments in terms of the church and its ministries. We've acknowledged them publicly and offered them to God in prayer. I've sensed real feelings of release in those moments. They've offered for some of us opportunities to mourn and grieve over things we long for still and for others the opportunity to grieve over not being listened to when we offered a new idea or tried something never done before.

In the action of grieving and release, we come together to grieve those memories that get in the way of our moving ahead, those things we didn't do, and the harboring of angry feelings because our ideas weren't listened to. We say the words we need to say to each other, and we ask that God would release us from our bondage. Observing these moments with symbols and gestures in addition to our words is helpful. Such acts as writing the griefs on pieces of paper (for some they still may be too painful to express out loud) and burning them or putting them in a trash can or forming our offerings into a litany with a corporate response of "Release us, O God," and singing a hymn can help us complete the action of grieving and release.

Reflect and act on the following:

1. Write down or share with another person what you mourn regarding the teaching ministry of your church.

2. Together decide on a symbolic way to acknowledge your grief before God and ask for release.

3. Sing or recite the words of a hymn such as "Renew Thy Church, Her Ministries Restore" (words by Kenneth L. Cober, tune "All Is Well").

Thanksgiving

Not only do we carry limiting memories and disappointments with us, we all too often fail to recognize the good that we do, or the things that are working, and stop and give thanks to God. Often it takes someone from outside to see and affirm what's working. We get so caught up in the doing and perhaps in thinking that what we are doing surely can't be important in the overall scheme of things.

I'm continually amazed by the teaching ministry and programs going on in the churches that I visit and hear about. We underestimate our own abilities and potential for renewing the teaching ministry of the church. There are signs of renewal in many congregations that I've visited. We need to identify the signs of renewal in our own congregations and in churches throughout the nation, publicly recognize them when the community is gathered for worship or fellowship, and give thanks to God for the creativity of the creators, the abilities of those who carry them out, and the difference they can make and are making in the lives of people. And in those places where we are struggling to provide meaningful ministries and programs and can only begin to ask the questions, we would give thanks as well. Formulating those questions is a first step.

Wouldn't it be wonderful if gratitude were in our hearts and on our tongues for all we attempt in the name of the teaching ministry of the church of Jesus Christ? Let's start by giving thanks to God for the small things.

Reflect and act on the following:

1. List all the parts of your church's teaching ministry that are working well.

2. List the two things about your church's teaching ministry of which you are most proud.

3. Combine your "thanksgivings" with those of others in the group. Make a litany using all these prayer offerings.

These six actions aren't comprehensive in terms of what the church is called to be regarding its teaching ministry. They really only offer us some guidance for finding our way in this wilderness time. Without clarity of mission and vision for how that mission can be accomplished in the future, we will continue to wander. And so it's to mission and vision that we turn next.

Chapter 2

Seeing Our Destination More Clearly

When you cross over the Jordan into the land of Canaan, . . . You shall take possession of the land and settle in it, for I have given you the land to possess.
—Numbers 33:51b,53

Write the vision; make it plain on tablets, so that a runner may read it. For there is still a vision for the appointed time.
—Habakkuk 2:2b-3a

Moses, with the help of God and Aaron, kept the mission before the Israelites. It wasn't an easy job. The Israelites complained, didn't trust the Lord, rebelled, skirted the hill country, and so forth. Still Moses kept the task he was charged with before them. In a similar fashion Jesus kept the mission before the disciples: "Go therefore and make disciples of all nations, baptizing them in the name of the Father and of the Son and of the Holy Spirit, and teaching them to obey everything that I have commanded you" (Matthew 28:19-20a).

We, too, are charged with keeping our mission clearly before us and with having a vision for how that mission can be carried out now and in the future. While the mission remains constant, the vision may change. In this wilderness time in the teaching ministry of the church, we are called to review our mission and to be sure the whole congregation understands and is able to articulate it so that even guests among us understand it. We can't, however, stop when we have a commonly understood and held mission. We must bring it to life with an accompanying vision for carrying out the mission in today's world and in the century that lies just ahead. And we must see it as part and parcel of the total ministry of the congregation. We cannot view it in isolation from the rest of the life and ministries of the church. Working on the mission of the church's teaching ministry must be done in consort with the overall mission of a congregation.

Mission and vision often are used interchangeably. So before we go any further, let's stop and briefly check some meanings. I like to think of *mission* in the following ways: the basic reason for a ministry's or program's existence, "why" a ministry or program exists, the basic purpose of a ministry or program. A statement of mission stands the test of time. It's long-term. I understand *vision* as a description of how the mission will be accomplished in the future. Offering direction for the future, vision is a clear image of a preferable future. Vision has a future focus, but it can also change so that one's mission can be accomplished in a new day and age.

In the pages that follow in this chapter we will look further at mission and vision because both are critical to finding our way in the wilderness and in finding new paths for the church's teaching ministry. We'll explore further meanings of the words and examples of each, as well as ways to help us review and clarify our mission and gain vision for the future.

Mission

Many of us may be more familiar with the word *purpose* than *mission*, and if you find it helpful, use *purpose* as a substitute. A mission, or purpose, statement clearly defines the task with which a group is charged. It speaks about core values and key beliefs. For those of us who care deeply about the teaching ministry of the church, our mission statement needs to clearly state the task with which we are charged, our core values, and key beliefs. To begin, let's turn to the Bible and refresh our minds about some of the things said there about the church's teaching ministry.

Keep these words that I am commanding you today in your heart. Recite them to your children and talk about them when you are at home and when you are away, when you lie down and when you rise. (Deuteronomy 6:6-7)

Go therefore and make disciples of all nations, baptizing them in the name of the Father and of the Son and of the Holy Spirit, and teaching them to obey everything that I have commanded you. (Matthew 28:19-20a)

. . . to equip the saints for the work of ministry, for building up the body of Christ, until all of us come to the unity of the faith and of the knowledge of the Son of God, to maturity, to the measure of the full stature of Christ. (Ephesians 4:12-13)

A mission statement talks about *why.* Such a statement can help us do several things: set clear goals and objectives, evaluate programs and activities, focus resources faithfully and effectively, quickly explain what we're about, determine priorities, and get and keep everyone on track. It doesn't have to be lengthy or wordy. In fact, many people believe that a mission statement should be brief and avoid jargon, and that it should be believable and understandable by folks both inside and outside the organization. It should emphasize the *why* rather than the *what* or *how*. There is no one way to write a mission statement; there is no right or wrong way to do it, as shown in the examples that follow:

Whole foods for healthy living, direct from America's original organic farm. (Walnut Acres)

Our Creed: To give you such outstanding quality, value, service and guarantee that we may be worthy of your high esteem. (Eddie Bauer)

Direct merchants. Guaranteed period. (Lands' End)

Welcomes all to a Christian environment of natural beauty, hospitality and acceptance. Through experiences of training, worship, fellowship and recreation, persons are refreshed, renewed and transformed for their journey of life and service. (a conference center in the Midwest)

A conference and retreat center for human development. (a center in Connecticut)

Educational Ministries, working with partners:
• *assists, encourages, and challenges congregations to become vital and faithful teaching/learning mission communities;*
• *calls and nurtures disciples of Jesus Christ to become change agents of God's reconciling love;*
• *prepares and supports committed lay and professional leaders for effective and creative ministry in the church and God's changing world. (Educational Ministries of the American Baptist Churches in the U.S.A.)*

To help you state or clarify the mission of your teaching ministry, you will find three tools in the back of this book: a suggested process to use (Appendix A), a list of ten purposes for a church's teaching ministry (Appendix B), and a checklist to see how your statement stacks up against some suggested criteria (Appendix C). When you have completed your work on a mission statement or feel comfortable with it, move on to develop your vision for your church's teaching ministry in the years ahead. Then you will have two important ingredients for paving the way into the future.

Vision

Let's review some things about the meaning of vision. George Barna, in *The Power of Vision: How You Can Capture and Apply God's Vision for Your Ministry,* suggests that vision is "foresight with insight based on hindsight." Or put another way, it is "seeing the invisible and making it visible."[1] Vision can provide the bridge across the span of wilderness into the future. Thinking about vision as a bridge is helpful to me. It suggests that there is a way or ways to be faithful and effective in the church's teaching ministry in order to come through this wilderness time. It provides hope when I'm most discouraged.

A vision for the future gives legs to a mission statement. It moves us from the past into the present and points us to the future. But there are some things that easily thwart or kill vision. We all have experienced one or more of them and even find them within ourselves. One of those deterrents is tradition as often expressed in words like, "We have a perfectly good way of doing that" or "We've always done it this way." A second deterrent is fear. We think we or the program might fail or that we might lose control. Another killer of vision is complacency expressed in words such as "It'll take too much time" or "Why bother?" Fatigue might be another killer. We and others are tired and burned out from all we are asked to do or all that we take on. Our own short-term thinking can be a block sometimes. We want quick results, tangible benefits. This may be the case more often than not in this era of fast-food restaurants, microwaves, and almost instant electronic communication. A "copycat" mentality can also thwart vision. Before copying what another church is doing, consider carefully the value and appropriateness for your congregation.

When people move beyond the blocks, they come up with vision statements such as the following:

A man on the moon by the end of the decade.
(John Kennedy)

A personal computer in every home that everyone can use.
(Bill Gates)

A place for people to find happiness and knowledge.
(Walt Disney)

Educational Ministries will be recognized for:
- *leadership in Christian religious education and publishing;*
- *mobilizing people to produce timely, results-oriented, innovative responses to ongoing and emerging educational needs in our congregations;*
- *managing its financial resources well. (Educational Ministries of the American Baptist Churches in the U.S.A.)*

When writing a vision statement, keep the following criteria in mind: (1) describe it in terms of the future; (2) state it clearly and in a compelling way—so that someone who didn't help write it can understand and commit himself or herself to it; (3) use vivid language, and make it motivational; and (4) keep it short. Defining and implementing a vision do not happen overnight. It takes time—time for prayer and discernment, time for planning, and time to build a base of support among members of a congregation.

You will find a process for developing a vision in Appendix D in the back of this book. As with the appendices related to writing a mission statement, it is assumed that the initiating body for shaping a vision for the teaching ministry of a congregation is the board or committee of Christian education and that there is general recognition that vision for the teaching ministry is an integral part of the whole. Work on vision needs to be coordinated with similar work for other aspects of the life of the congregation. The process that is described in Appendix D takes five to six hours to complete. It can be done at a weekend retreat or in three separate two-hour sessions. The core group of participants needs to be the board of Christian education with additional representatives from the larger congregation. Ideally these representatives will reflect the diversity within the congregation.

The key to vision is being in tune with God's vision for the teaching ministry of your congregation. Discerning God's will becomes singularly important, and there's no one or simple way to go about that discernment. Praying together is a good place to begin, however. Concentrate on what God's future might be. Spend time in quiet listening. Be attentive to what God is calling your congregation's teaching ministry to be and do. In chapter 3 we will consider how some congregations are seeking to respond to God's vision for teaching in these times.

Chapter 3

Trying New Paths

Then the LORD said to me: "You have been skirting
this hill country long enough. Head north, and
charge the people as follows." —*Deuteronomy 2:2-4a*

For many of us a nudge is needed in order to risk trying
something new. In that way we are not unlike the Israelites,
who needed a push from God in order to head north. We may
need the same kind of push from God to try some new ways.
I'm encouraged by the number of churches that are trying new
ways—big and small. In addition, there are many churches
asking key questions about what they are currently doing and
wondering out loud if there aren't some other ways to do
things. Posing the questions is a good beginning for risking
change. We need to give attention to our questions and those
of others. Such questions include: Is this what God would
have us do? What might be some other ways to fulfill our
mission? Are we clear about our mission? What is God's
vision for our teaching ministry at the turn of the century?
Which churches are trying some innovative ways of doing
Christian education? What other ways might work for us in
this situation? What and how are we called to teach faithfully
in this day and age? How can we make a difference in the
lives of children, youth, and adults?

Churches are trying new ways for a variety of reasons.
Some have been frustrated by small and/or irregular attendance,
discipline challenges, or difficulty in recruiting teachers and

leaders. Others have sought to respond to specific needs within the church or larger community. Many of these churches have found themselves in changing communities whose needs are often quite different from the needs of the membership of the church itself. Still some have been motivated by their reading of Scripture and observations of today's culture to try some new and hopefully faithful ways. In a pluralistic, materialistic, and often violent world we want our teaching to make a difference; we want people to be transformed and transforming Christians.

Theological Reflections on Changes

While I believe it is important to discern what God's vision is for our teaching ministries as we begin a new century, that concern may not always be our starting point for making changes. The place we start is not as important as making sure that at some point in the process we stop and listen to what God is saying to us about our plans. We need to stop and do some critical reflection. Some of our questions will have to do with whether or not what we're planning is practical or economical or educationally sound or demographically or sociologically appropriate.

Thinking theologically about the changes we seek is also important. Theological questions are priority questions that ought not to be passed over. They can help us reflect on the meaning of a change. They can help us determine if the change is being made in relationship with God's presence and purpose. They can help us see if we are on target faithwise. They are at the core of bringing about faithful change in the church's teaching ministry.

Using questions such as the following can help us reflect on the change we're seeking to bring about or evaluate a change we've made:

How is the biblical message communicated in this change?

What biblical message is communicated?

How does this change help the congregation build community? help individuals and the congregation make faith meaningful in their lives? help nurture Christian hope?

In what ways does this change promote inclusion as in "we are all one in Christ"?

What does this change communicate about who God is for this community? about the relationship of individuals and this community to Jesus Christ? about who the church is and what the church is called to be and do? about the role of the Bible for this community? about the power of the Holy Spirit in this community?

How does this change help individuals and the community remember who they are as people of God, who they are called to be, and what they are called to do in the future?

How is God perceived at work in this change?

What does this change teach about human beings before God?

What biblical images come to mind as you explore this change?

These or similar questions could be developed into a checklist to use in considering and comparing several options for new ways of doing Christian education or in evaluating changes that have already been made.

Reflect and act on the following:

Pause now, reflect on the list above, and add some theological questions of your own. Then test some of the questions.

Many churches, after wondering what to do with their Christian education program and perhaps delaying any action, have decided to try new paths, new directions. They are experimenting with ways of doing Christian education that are new for them. Some of the changes could be called foundational; others are just a course correction or slightly different change in approach. As I've learned about many of these new ways, I found myself cataloging them into the two broad categories of *adaptive change* and *foundational change*. Adaptive changes include using alternate times and settings, having an emphasis on small groups, building a teaching ministry around special days and events, and one-on-one teaching. Foundational changes include programming with attention to the boundaries people are crossing in their lives; intergenerational programming; seeing congregational life as teaching, especially with education and worship being connected or education and mission or education and social action; and organizing to educate people for faithful ministry at home, work or school, and community—what often is called *ministry of the laity*. Let's look at some specific examples of these two kinds of changes.

Adaptive Changes

Adaptive changes are more in the nature of adjustments. We make adjustments so that what we are doing better fits the culture or situation in which we find ourselves. One way of looking at such changes is to see them as adapting the point or place where ministry meets the culture. One such adaptive change is a change in time or setting.

One church made such a change. It moved from a Sunday morning educational program for children and youth to a midweek after-school program. Other churches have moved church school from Sunday morning to Saturday morning, thereby reaching children and youth in surrounding neighborhoods who didn't come on Sunday for a variety of reasons, including not being able to dress in the way they assumed was expected. A new church start meets in another congregation's building and holds its worship in the early evening on Sundays, preceded by its educational program at 4:00 P.M. The congregation is small, and the program includes a club-type group for children ages 3 through sixth grade, a senior-high youth group, and an adult Bible study group.

Some churches have developed a pattern of organizing some of their Christian education programming around special events and days, often following the church year. During Advent and Lent they gather for special programs that may bring together the entire Sunday church school, often doing something intergenerationally. One small city church plans a change of pace on Christian education Sunday. The director of Christian education works with the young people in planning an educational experience with all of the children together in one room, thus freeing teachers of children to join other teachers and adults for a special program just for adults. Outside speakers are sometimes invited. An event such as this provides a time of enrichment and often training for teachers, an experience in leadership for youth, and a change of pace for children.

Another church has instituted what they are calling Sabbath Sundays. They occur periodically and take the place of the regular Sunday church school. All classes come together for an educational experience that is often light and fun. These Sabbath Sundays are planned by a small group, not Sunday church school teachers, thus giving teachers a rest. Frequently they take place on a special day in the church year, such as Pentecost. An urban congregation sought a change in order to integrate two developmentally challenged students into the Sunday church school. Two public school special-education teachers volunteered to be with the students in their regular classes so that they wouldn't have to be separated from the others or be in a special class provided just for them.

Other churches have begun to use small groups for adults at many and varied times other than Sunday morning or in addition to that time of week. The groups can be just for men or just for women, just for young adults or just for older adults. Sometimes they are focused on particular topics of interest; sometimes they are covenantal Bible study groups or ministry groups. Sometimes the entire congregation is divided into small cell groups. The possibilities are almost endless. One suburban church has focused on some groups for women including a group for young mothers and a journaling group. Usually such small groups require a commitment to regular attendance for the duration of the group. In that sense they are covenantal. Note that some approaches to the use of small groups in a church's teaching ministry may be more of a foundational change than an adaptive one.

Foundational Changes

Foundational changes are more than an adjustment in time or setting or age grouping. Foundational changes are those that reorder the purpose and reason for being of the educational program, that change how and why something is done in a fundamental way or at a fundamental level. They are changes made at the core or center of a church's teaching ministry. In our day and age foundational changes may be more needed if our teaching ministries are to impact lives and communities in significant ways. Foundational changes do operate at a different level and can be made along with adaptive changes. Foundational changes tend to focus on things previously overlooked, to view education in a radically different way, to meet the needs of people not usually involved, and/or to bring together people quite different from one another.

Many churches are seeking to integrate the teaching ministry into the total life of the congregation. They view teaching as a part of all that is done. They see the congregation as needing to teach and to be taught. They also assume that teaching is the responsibility of the entire congregation, not just of those teaching or leading the Sunday church school.

One place where this is seen most clearly is in congregations where education and worship are being integrated. One congregation has been intentional about connecting its worship and educational programming. This meant changing worship from 10:00 to 11:00 A.M. so Sunday school could precede worship. The pastor uses the lectionary to organize worship and preaching, and the same texts are used in the Sunday church school. Their lectionary-based curriculum has helped them make this connection.[1] Such connecting needs the commitment, planning, and involvement of the pastor(s) and laypeople. In the case of this church, the pastor's involvement in teaching grades 4-6 was significant. He says, "Teaching the children was one of the best things I've done in ministry because it gave me the Sunday school teacher's perspective on what it was like to teach all year in the Sunday school with little connection to what was going on in worship."[2]

The change in this church was not made without tensions; however, it did help to decrease a certain sense of isolation that many teachers had felt. And recruitment of Sunday school teachers, which had been a problem before, became easier. Moreover, Sunday school has become a preparatory stage for worship. The pastor reports that "the integration of worship and education has been a great blessing, and we continue to try to meet its challenges, relying on prayer and God's grace."[3]

A church in a small college town, guided by a concept developed by the pastor, tried an intergenerational Sunday church school. A few of the pastor's words from the introduction of his proposal set the scene.

As a pastor and as a parent I have given a lot of thought to Christian education in general and to Sunday school in particular. We need to decide how God would have us answer one question when it comes to Christian education.

The question is this. What sort of people does God seek to emerge from a sound approach to Christian education?
. . .

As I look at our Sunday School program, I am impressed by the number of people involved and their love for Jesus Christ. For twelve years I have sensed frustration on the part of dedicated men and women as they have tried to make an "age-graded" process work in inferior facilities with curriculum that may or may not apply to the children. What this approach seems to achieve is a basic understanding of nine or so Bible stories in the course of eight years. I don't think I've ever seen a person come through this approach who could apply the Bible effectively to life. What they know of Christian character they have achieved in spite of the curriculum, through the example of the fine Christians who teach them.

Frankly, I think we are kidding ourselves if we think the Sunday School is doing all that God would have us do in an educational ministry. We are selling ourselves and our children short in a world caught in the turmoil of spiritual warfare. In this climate, why are we copying (and doing it poorly) the approach our kids experience with increasing frustration at school? The time has come for careful thought, prayer, and for new directions. I submit this perspective and proposal as a "statement in principle" and a "tentative framework" from which to work.[4]

A core group of laypeople worked with the pastor in developing the idea and in adapting curriculum resources. Adults were given the option of being involved in the intergenerational program or in one adult class that would continue to be offered. Initially separate programming was planned for children from infancy through kindergarten. Primary-grade children were included in the intergenerational programming, but after a few weeks it was decided to provide separate programming for them as well. During the time designated for church school, small intergenerational groups met for study of a particular Bible passage and activities. On some Sundays, all small groups gathered for a time together.

Developing curriculum resources, while extremely beneficial to those individuals, proved to be time-consuming. While the pastor took the lead in the change, laypeople came on board early and gained ownership in the idea and plans. One indication of the level of lay ownership was the time they met without the pastor and decided his suggestion for a curriculum topic wouldn't work. They came up with their own idea and fondly referred to that moment as the time they mutinied! The congregation moved from an intergenerational Sunday church school when several key leaders died or moved away and when children and youth indicated they missed peer groups.

One federated church has organized its congregational life around ministry in the home, at work, and in the community. Worship, education, and even the administrative structure of the church are fashioned with this lay-ministry approach in mind. A single mother speaks sincerely about what this has meant for her as a parent and mother. On a Sunday when the ministry of parenting or mothering (or fathering) is being lifted up, symbols of this ministry are placed at the front of the sanctuary, and parents are prayed for. Think of the teaching that is happening in the sanctuary on such a Sunday!

Yet another church, a small congregation, has a study group of adults meeting with adults from a nearby synagogue. All of them are gaining new understandings as they meet across religious faith lines.

Some churches are seeking to reorder the way mission, ministry, and work are done. They have moved to ministry teams rather than traditional committees. They, along with others that have chosen to keep the traditional organization, are seeking to think about persons in leadership roles as more than bodies filling an office for a specified term; that is, they are thinking of such persons as spiritual leaders. With this view, they recognize that time needs to be given at each meeting to pray and be guided spiritually and to learn what it means to be a spiritual leader in the congregation and in the community in this day and age. In this way meeting times take on an educational and spiritual development role as well as a ministry planning and implementing role.

Reflect and act on the following:

Think about the changes you wish or need to make in the teaching ministry of your church. Then reflect and act on the following:

1. How would you classify the changes you think should be made?

2. Use the theological questions listed earlier in the chapter, or some of your own, to help you assess the changes.

3. Invite others to join you in the assessment.

Remember that it is all right to experiment, to try something without making a long-term commitment, without the plan being set in stone—yet giving it a long enough time to be known and take hold. Learning and other possibilities often grow out of changes that don't work as planned. So it's even okay to fail and learn from the failure!

Remember, too, that we are not alone. God promises over and over again to be with us. We have many partners in the teaching ministry who share similar concerns and joys. Give thanks for God's presence and the partnership of many people committed to the church's teaching ministry.

We will consider more about partnerships in chapter 5. Meanwhile let's think about what teaching looks like during this wilderness time in the church's teaching ministry.

Chapter 4

Teaching along the Way

. . . things that we have heard and known,
  that our ancestors have told us.
We will not hide them from their children;
  we will tell to the coming generation
the glorious deeds of the LORD,
and his might,
  and the wonders that he has done.
                        —Psalm 78:3-4

In this wilderness time in the teaching ministry of the
church, teaching does and must go on. The *biblical story* must
be told. And it is and can be told in faithful and creative ways
even as we experiment and seek direction for new ways for
the ministry to which it is central.

Let's first refresh our memories about the meaning of
teaching and teacher. Jesus was a teacher—a rabbi. He taught
using stories and parables and questions (Luke 10:25-37, for
example). He was attentive to his audience (Luke 9:10-17).
He spoke and acted with authority, most often outside the
synagogue (Luke 6:17-49). Historically, rabbis in the Jewish
community were the principal teachers for communal male
education on the advanced level and were often the supervi-
sors of education. The key vehicles used by the rabbis were
Scripture, communal worship, and holidays and commemo-
rative occasions. Much of the activity in the synagogue

centered on education.[1] Jesus, then, in many ways offered a new model of teacher and teaching.

One contemporary definition of a teacher is "an instructor whose duty is to impart knowledge about a particular subject following a systematic, methodical procedure."[2] When it comes to teaching the Christian faith, such a definition is incomplete. In teaching faith we are called not only to share information about the faith; we are to proclaim the faith as our own and challenge and encourage students to respond to these truths in their own lives. This is done in both formal and informal ways. We have people formally designated as teachers in the Christian education programs of our churches. We know that many persons of faith, including parents and guardians, are informal teachers of the faith. We can't ignore this informal teaching because we know that the Christian faith is both "caught" and "taught."

But this chapter is intended to address formal teaching in the congregation. That's not to say that the informal teaching is unimportant. It's not. Indeed, it is vitally important in any community of faith. Congregations need to give more attention to the many opportunities for informal teaching that regularly present themselves and to equip members to be alert to and equipped for those opportunities. Informal teaching does need to be addressed but in some other place, at some other time.[3]

This chapter does not seek to address specific models, styles, or approaches of teaching; rather it seeks to address ten tasks that seem appropriate for this in-between time. They are tasks for all teachers within the faith community no matter the age taught. It is assumed that key leaders in a church's teaching ministry will encourage and help teachers in these tasks and will hold them accountable. In today's world a teaching partnership is required. Those responsible for administering a congregation's teaching ministry must stand with teachers and support them.

Let's consider the ten tasks. I would encourage you to add other tasks that you believe are important for teachers in your congregation today. Make your own list or add yours in the space provided at the end of the chapter.

Being a Companion on the Journey with Students

This may seem obvious. However, I believe we often forget that our own Christian faith journeys continue. They are not completed. We, too, are faith works in progress. Why not acknowledge this to those we teach? Why not approach the teaching ministry as a learner, too? Before God both students and teachers are learners; both are created in God's image; and both are companions with the one who creates, redeems, and sustains each of us.

For some of us acknowledging to students our continuing journey can be a freeing experience. It can free us from having to know all the answers and from not always living up to expectations that either we or students hold of us. We can say openly and without fear that God is not done with us yet.

Acknowledging that we are a companion on the faith journey with students teaches that learning the Christian faith is a lifelong task. There is always room for growth. Such companionship models both a style of teaching and a style of faith worth emulating. Even teachers continue on the journey of faith.

Being a companion on the faith journey with students means giving attention to one's own spiritual needs and gifts—keeping an inventory, if you will. The inventory need not be so much a structured list written down at set intervals as much as being aware of areas of one's faith needing attention and doing something about them. But if you are a list maker like I am, you may want to write down the inventory and identify certain times when you will make assessments. Keeping an inventory requires stopping to rest from the activity of teaching and listening to God's voice. Keeping an inventory requires prayer and reflection, times of quiet. Keeping an inventory requires personal assessment. It may require the assistance of other persons who can both encourage and challenge you to take needed steps in strengthening your spiritual development. Some Christian education leaders have found a spiritual growth group or a spiritual director to be helpful.[4]

Providing Hospitality

The God of grace and glory that we serve is a hospitable God and encourages us to be the same, particularly in our teaching. Our hospitality is made possible because this hospitable God we worship and serve invites us to treat others in like manner.

Images of hospitality weave a strong thread of welcome throughout the biblical story. Beginning with the twists and turns of the Hebrew people's wilderness wanderings, our ancestors in the faith were always seeking places of rest and safety, places of unconditional welcome where hosts waited to hear their stories and receive their gifts. Some of the images that come to mind are a woman of Shunem furnishing a rooftop shelter for Elisha's comfort; Mary and Martha opening their home to Jesus; a rich man inviting the poor, the crippled, and the blind to his banquet; a Samaritan kneeling to care for a wounded man others had ignored; a compassionate father running to put his arms around his son who was returning from a distant country.

We, too, are called to create safe and comfortable places, to welcome guests (students), to listen to our guests' stories and share our own, and to encourage students to move into the world with words of blessing and acts of inclusion because they have been welcomed. Havens and safe places are more and more important in the world in which we live. Children need to be in safe environments where they won't be hurt or abused and where they can play and learn in peace. Youth and adults need to feel that they can share openly and honestly and that what is shared does not leave that place. Hospitable places respect and honor both guests and hosts, both students and teachers.

Dorothy Day offers a helpful perspective on hospitality:

For a total Christian, the goad of duty is not needed—always prodding one to perform this or that good deed. It is not a duty to help Christ, it is a privilege. Is it likely that Martha and Mary sat back and considered that they had done all that was expected of them—is it likely that Peter's mother-in-law grudgingly served the chicken she had meant to keep till Sunday because she thought it was her "duty"? She did it gladly; she would have served ten chickens if she had them.

If that is the way they gave hospitality to Christ, it is certain that is the way it should still be given. Not for the sake of humanity. Not because it might be Christ who stays with us, comes to see us, takes up our time. Not because these people remind us of Christ . . . but because they are Christ, asking us to find room for Him, exactly as He did at the first Christmas.[5]

Giving Attention to Thresholds in People's Lives

This task in many ways is a reminder that most people are more open to learnings and teachings of faith at special times in their lives. We sometimes speak of "teachable or kairos moments." We can even list some such thresholds, such as when a child is born, a child starts school, an infant or child is dedicated or baptized, a youth graduates from high school, someone graduates from college, someone is married, a person gets a first job, someone loses a job, a loved one dies, someone is seriously ill, someone is divorced, and so forth.

But these may be the more obvious thresholds. We are

charged with the task of giving attention to those we teach so that we come to know their needs and gifts and can sense teachable moments—or at least listening moments. We can tune our eyes and ears to hear and see the bad days at school or work, the hurtful times with other kids, the abuse and/or neglect at home, prejudice and hatred, a radical change in lifestyle. We can know the moments of joy and excitement, when honors are bestowed or good news is received.

Planning and carrying out our teaching plans need to be done with these and other thresholds of our students in mind. As we prepare sessions, we can pause and reflect on the life situation, needs, and gifts of each of our students and seeking to make connections between those life situations and the content of the session that we are preparing. We are called to stand at the entry and help people cross the threshold. We'll also be better prepared to change the session plan if the life experience of one or more students requires such flexibility.

And as we teach, we listen with our ears, our eyes, and our total being—giving full attention to those present. In our listening we are careful not to jump to conclusions about the cause of someone's behavior. We make ourselves available to learn more, to be ready to listen if someone wants to confide, to intervene if such action is called for, or to celebrate when the occasion is right.

Respecting All Persons

The Bible speaks about hallowing God in the Lord's Prayer (Matthew 6:9) and about honoring God in other places. In several places in the Scripture accounts, we could substitute "respecting God" for "honoring God." It seems to me that we are called to hallow and honor and respect each other as well. God respects and honors and hallows us, and we are created in God's image. God's respect knows no limits, nor should ours.

Unless we respect ourselves, it is unlikely that we can

respect others. So again we are called to begin with ourselves, to look at ourselves respectfully so that we might teach others with respect.

While we come with authority to the teaching task, we are no better than those we teach. We have authority because we have been called by God. And because our authority comes from God, we cannot lord it over students. We can't punish them or abuse them or shame them or manipulate them. They also have been called or will be called by God for a ministry.

Romans 12:10 suggests a motto for us: "Love one another with mutual affection; outdo one another in showing honor."

Granting Freedom yet Making the Boundaries Clear

It seems to me that it is easy to swing one way or the other when it comes to freedom and boundaries. What does seem important is the proper balance between granting freedom and making boundaries clear. The kind of relationship between these two stances no doubt will vary depending on the people, culture, and group we find ourselves teaching. Boundaries of some sort are important to most people. The nature and kind of boundary will differ from person to person or group to group. Groups, like individuals, have lives of their own. People and groups often have to grow into freedom; thus, we begin with stronger boundaries and then loosen up. Sometimes the boundaries are strengthened again near the close of an experience.

When we teach young children, we might well set the boundary that any structure they build with the wooden blocks may be no higher than their heads. Some students, especially youth, will test the boundaries, but that does not necessarily mean that the boundary is not needed. The testing may instead be a way of seeking a boundary. Being aware of that possibility ahead of time can prepare us if and when it happens. When inviting adults to share personal experiences, we might say that it is all right to pass, thus letting adults set their own boundaries.

And when granting freedom we need to remember our own boundaries. We need to be aware of our own limits, make these known, and ask that they be honored. They may need to be interpreted to students because each of us has different boundaries, and if students are used to one set of limits, they cannot be expected to automatically respond to a new set. For example, my tolerance for noise or sound may be less than another teacher's. Being up front about that from the start and explaining why can help the boundary be respected. And if there is a team of teachers working with students at different times, it is a good idea to talk about the limits and boundaries for the group and to arrive at some common standards.

Sharing and Encouraging
God's Story and Our Stories

Central to our teaching is the biblical story of God's relationship with human beings and the Good News of Jesus' life, death, and resurrection. We need to know that story just as we need to know our own story of faith and how the two connect. We need to be avid readers and students of the Book—no matter what the ages of students we teach, whether nursery twos and threes or senior adults. We need to be transformed by the message of the Bible and recognize the power of the message for others. It's not enough to know the biblical story and our own story in relationship to it; we also need to share both stories as we teach and to encourage students to learn about God's work throughout history as revealed in Scripture so that they can see their own life stories in relationship to that story.

For the biblical story to be fresh continually, we need to regularly read the Scriptures and not just the familiar and favorite passages. We need to be challenged anew by the unfamiliar and difficult passages. Some things that might help in keeping the Word fresh are occasionally reading the Bible from cover to cover, deliberately reading from a variety of translations, auditing a seminary Bible course, or being part of a covenantal Bible study group—all in addition to the Scripture reading we do as part of our teaching preparation.

Throughout Scripture we are called to share the biblical story with others. One place is Psalm 105:1, 2b, 5.

> O give thanks to the LORD, call on his name,
>   make known his deeds among the peoples.
>   . . .
>   tell of all his wonderful works.
>   . . .
> Remember the wonderful works he has done,
>   his miracles, and the judgments he uttered.

Preparing People to Be Involved in the Church's Life and Mission

We need to see that part of what we are doing as we teach is preparing people to take their places in the life and mission of the church as lived out in the local congregation and its surrounding community. If we teach in isolation from the rest of the faith community, we are not only missing a great opportunity, but we are also continuing to propagate an individualistic faith. The Christian faith is a communal faith. We are called to prepare people to become faith members of the Christian community and to help them to be a part of the total life of the community.

The key for teachers in the church today is preparing students for corporate worship and for participation in mission. Of course, this means involvement in worship and mission ourselves. We teach by example, and we teach when we tell students why it is we participate in corporate worship and mission projects. It also means teaching children, youth, and adults new to the faith the Lord's Prayer, the Doxology, and other parts of a worship service that most of us have committed to memory. Knowing the words, the songs, and what's expected are basic to feeling that one belongs to this worshiping people. Having the basics well in hand frees us to worship God in the service.

Mission involvement doesn't stop with involvement in service projects, as important as they are. It includes working for justice for all and sensing our call to be ministers of the gospel at work, at home, at school, and in the community. It begins in small, immediate, and concrete ways with young children right within the classroom and the church building and extends for older youth and adults into the community and the world beyond.

Reflecting with Students on Their Experiences in the Church's Life and Mission

Preparing for involvement in the community of faith is only part of what's required of us. We also need to help students reflect on their experiences in the life and mission of the congregation. This, it would seem, is more often neglected than the preparation. We all can be helped to reflect and learn from our life experiences whether within the community of faith or outside of it.

Such time for reflection could occur at the beginning or end of each Sunday church school or weekday study session. Reflection can be built into both worship and mission projects. Pause for people to speak briefly about their experiences the past week in the church, at home, at work or in school, and so forth, about where they make connections between their faith and life experience, about how we can support one another, and about the difference that is being made in the name of Christ.

Some of the theological questions posed in chapter 3 can be helpful here as well.

How was the biblical message communicated in this experience?

How was God at work in this experience?

What Bible story comes to mind as a result of this experience?

How did this experience help you remember who you are and what you are called to do as a Christian?

How did this experience help build Christian community? make the meaning of faith clearer in your life? nurture Christian hope?

Trying New Ways of Teaching

What better opportunity is there than such a time as this to try some new ways of teaching—not for the sake of our own teaching but for the sake of reaching students? Ask yourself to what extent you might be stuck in a rut. Are you reaching only some of the students when a change in methodology or the offering of choices would mean reaching more? Assess your teaching methods and style. Ask yourself, What's working? effective? faithful? What new or additional ways might be the breakthrough in reaching a student you are concerned about?

One way to determine which new ways might be most appropriate is to list students by name and beside each name to jot down the ways in which that student best learns. Teachers may need to observe students more closely for several sessions and then note their preferred learning styles. With older students it's a good idea to check out your assumptions with them. You also might want to review chapter 3 of this book for the bigger picture or read a book about learning styles and appropriate teaching methods.

Changing teaching ways or methods just for the sake of

new methods may help us get out of a teaching rut, but it isn't student centered. Knowing how the specific students we teach learn best is the important factor here.

Giving Thanks

The Bible admonishes us to give thanks to God in all things; that includes our teaching, both on the good days and the bad days. Begin with yourself. Make an attitude adjustment, if necessary. Consider practicing saying a prayer of thanksgiving at the end of each class or group session or each day for a different person in your class. Work to make giving thanks become a habit of your heart. Start each day with a prayer of thanksgiving to God for all that's good in your life and for the strength to face the things that aren't so good.

Model such thanksgiving in class with your students. Give them opportunities to express thanks to God. Help them practice giving thanks with regularity so they, too, might make thanksgiving a habit of the heart.

As I work on developing a lifestyle of gratitude, I'm frequently reminded of the closing sentence of a prayer of thanksgiving offered before a clergy luncheon that I attended, "And let us not complain." We need to complain less and give thanks more. We can begin by making small incremental moves from complaining to thanksgiving in our daily lives. Again, our example and our testimony for giving thanks will be the teachers.

Use the space allotted here for making your own list of teaching tasks in this in-between time or for adding to the preceding list of ten tasks.

Encourage teachers to take stock of how well they are carrying out each of the ten tasks (or the list of tasks you may have developed). "Taking Stock," Appendix E at the back of the book, is an assessment tool that can be duplicated and used by teachers to take stock of themselves. Or you may wish to use another teacher assessment tool. There are others available, including one in *The Work of the Sunday School Superintendent*, which is listed in the resource section at the end of this book. Completed assessment tools such as these can be useful to a board of Christian education as it seeks to provide teacher training and support that meets the needs of teachers. So ahead of time ask teachers to share their self-assessments with the board.

Being called to teach others in the Christian community is a privilege and a gift. While it requires preparation and effort, it offers moments of real joy and fulfillment, and the good thing about it is that we are not alone. More about that in the next chapter.

Chapter 5

Journeying Not Alone

I have called you.—Isaiah 42:6a

I am about to do a new thing.—Isaiah 43:19a

Remember, I am with you always.—Matthew 28:20b

Most of us as teachers and Christian education leaders have had moments when we felt all alone—or at least discouraged—in our teaching ministry. What comes to mind for me is the very first Sunday church school class I ever taught. I grew up in a small church and was asked to teach when I was still a high school student. Most Sundays I felt like a complete failure at the end of the session with a very small group of primary children, dominated by two brothers. I had the feeling of going it all alone, and I didn't feel like a teacher in spite of the title given to me. It was years later before I could call myself "teacher." I am probably not alone. Many teachers feel isolated. Such feelings may contribute to teacher resignations and discouragement.

How can we claim God's presence for ourselves as we teach and/or give leadership in the church's teaching ministry? Most of us know teachers who teach with the assurance that they are not alone, that they have been called by God, that they are surrounded by God's presence and the support of many partners. They are confident. They teach or lead with authority. Being encouraged themselves, they encourage others. They believe that God is doing a new thing, and they are called to participate in that new thing. While they are rooted in the past, they teach or lead in the present with hope that they are making a difference for the future. Remembering who they are as people of faith, being present as teachers of the faith, and living in hope are all important to them.

Think for a moment about one such teacher or Christian education leader you know. Reflect on the following:

1. What are the signs that this person believes he or she is called to teach and that this person operates out of an understanding of the support of God and of many others?

2. What does this person do to claim God's presence and the support of others?

3. Who undergirds this person and how?

Now let's look at some ways that can help us claim God's presence in our lives as teachers or leaders, affirm our call, and be open to the new things to which God calls us. Responding to God's call to do new things usually means making changes. Changes require personal transformation and corporate transformation, which usually don't come without tension and struggle. Change is not always easy and doesn't happen overnight. Thus we need to give ourselves and others permission to struggle and be challenged. Compare your reflections on the questions above with the following ways to find personal support for your teaching ministry.

Personal Prayer

Spending regular time in prayer for yourself is important. Don't consider it selfish. Seek God's vision and direction for your teaching. Be silent and listen. Ask questions and have a dialogue. Setting aside a time each day can help this practice of prayer become a habit—something to rely on when the feelings of aloneness are about to grab hold. Then when the desperate moment comes, pause in the situation and ask God to take charge or to walk with you in a special way. Perhaps a set prayer can be of help in the most desperate moments. A request such as "Be my teacher now, O God," or "Grant me peace" may help when no words of your own can be prayed.

If you don't clearly sense a call to teach or lead, pray for clarity about your call. Perhaps the call will be clarified in the midst of your teaching or as you listen for understanding about whether or not your teaching-ministry assignment is what you're called to do at this time. As you pray for personal clarity and strength, lift up and encourage your teaching partners. You are not alone in this ministry, and your partners include not only other teachers but also students and folks within the congregation who don't teach but are committed to the teaching ministry of the church.

Prayer Partner

Having a person assigned to you as a prayer partner is a very tangible way of being supported and not feeling alone in your teaching ministry, whether it's teaching or Christian education administration. It is also a very visible means of mutual encouragement. Many churches have arranged for prayer partners for all teachers and/or classes. If your church has not arranged for prayer partners for teachers, suggest the idea to the board of Christian education or invite a friend to be your prayer partner. Inviting someone not involved in the teaching ministry in any way also has the possibility of broadening the base of support for your church's teaching ministry and interpreting its importance in the congregation's life and mission.

In one case a teacher of junior high students was having a difficult time. With the permission of the teacher, the board of Christian education in that church arranged for a shut-in in the congregation to be a prayer partner for this teacher. The prayer partner agreed to pray as the teacher prepared, during the class session, and following the session. Eventually the class became aware of this partnership, got acquainted with the prayer partner, and ministered to him. They learned that he had formerly taught junior high students. And the junior high teacher gained confidence in her teaching.

The idea of prayer partners can be extended to the entire congregation by including a specific teaching-ministry request in each Sunday morning prayer in corporate worship. What better way and time could there possibly be to ask that God's new things be made visible to the gathered congregation?

Teacher/Leader Support Group

Setting up a teacher support group is another way of helping teachers feel less lonely and of developing a system of mutual encouragement. Such a group would be voluntary and would establish for itself the frequency of meetings and any structure needed. The purpose of such a group would be to share joys and concerns and pray together—to encourage one another. The participants might even share resources from time to time or do Bible study together, perhaps during special seasons of the year, such as Lent.

A teacher/leader support group might explore the vocation of teaching, considering what it means to be called by God to teach. And what better group could explore new ways of doing things, new teaching methods, and how it is that God is making "a way in the wilderness" (Isaiah 43:19b)?

Mentor

As I think back on my first teaching experience in the church, I wish I'd had a teaching mentor—someone who might have walked with me as I began, someone to be my encourager, someone to whom I could address questions, concerns, frustrations. (I would add joys to the list, except I don't remember any joys in that experience!) Ideally this person would have met with me before I began teaching and as I prepared (giving me some clues for that as well), would have been present in the classroom as I taught, and would have been available afterward to reflect on the experiences. In addition, I would have felt free to call up this person and ask a question or share an idea. Such a mentor would have eased my feeling of going it alone.

Another possibility, which is similar to establishing mentors, is to assign a member of the board of Christian education to each teacher. This should be part of a church's covenant with teachers. This assignment identifies for the teacher a point of contact, a person to whom questions and concerns can be addressed. In turn, the board member takes on the responsibility of asking, "How's it going? How can the board of Christian education be of help?"

Learning from the Biographies of Faithful Teachers and Leaders

Check your church or public library for books on important teachers and leaders. Reading the life stories of teachers and leaders who have gone before you can provide insight and inspiration for your own growth as a teacher. I can think of several such biographies that have inspired me. You no doubt can think of others. On my list are *Teacher* by Sylvia Ashton Warner; *The Song Goes On: The Story of Ioleta Hunt McElhaney* by Claribel F. Dick; *Matriarch of Conspiracy, Ruth Von Kleist, 1867-1945* by Jane Pejsa; *To the Golden Shore: The*

Life of Adoniram Judson by Courtney Anderson; and *Walter Rauschenbusch: American Reformer* by Paul M. Minus.

As you read, note when and how these believers were called to their ministries, how they were encouraged and encouraged others, and what new things God revealed to them and helped them to do.

Interviews with Saints of the Church

Another angle on the biographies is to interview older members of the congregation who have previously taught in the Sunday church school. Here's an opportunity to understand their call to teach as well as to learn how they found support in the teaching task, what joys and concerns were present in their teaching days, and how they claimed God's presence in their teaching lives. Note how they were encouraged and encouraged others and what new things God revealed to them and helped them to do.

Teacher Training

Often training in teaching skills or understanding faith development can help one gain confidence in teaching. Such teacher training goes hand in hand with the ways described above. Developing self-confidence as a teacher is something I believe God wants for all teachers in the church's educational ministry. Strengthening the gifts God has given each of us can go a long way in making us feel that we are not alone and that someone cares enough to provide training.

Teacher training does not need to be limited to skill development or knowledge of faith development. Churches can offer sessions on understanding one's call to teach, being encouraged and encouraging others, and being open to new ways and approaches to the teaching ministry. Important to recognizing God's new things is an understanding of the culture and world in which we live. As the hymn suggests, "new occasions teach new duties" ("Once to Every Man and Nation").

Training can take place at several levels: local, regional, state, and national. Contact your denomination's regional or national offices for information on workshops, books and other resources, and events.

Take a moment to jot down in the space provided an outline for a support and nurture plan for yourself and for those who teach and give leadership in your church's teaching ministry. Incorporate any of the ideas mentioned in this chapter and ideas from your own well of resources.

Appendix F offers some steps to take in building a leader development plan for your congregation and includes an example of an outline for that type of plan. It has been developed, in part, to help leaders realize that today's Christian education wilderness does not need to overcome us. We have at our fingertips resources galore to help us find our way, to make the badly needed new maps. Think about it! We are called to be Christian education cartographers. The good news is we don't have to work alone. God calls us, is with us, and is making a new way. And we have the possibility of numerous partners—both those who have gone before and those present with us now—in mapping the future to which God calls us.

May this be our prayer: "Now may our Lord Jesus Christ himself and God our Father, who loved us and through grace gave us eternal comfort and good hope, comfort [our] hearts and strengthen them in every good work and word" (2 Thessalonians 2:16-17).

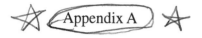 Appendix A

Developing a Mission Statement for the Teaching Ministry of a Congregation

These steps assume that the initiating body for the development of a mission statement for the teaching ministry of a congregation is the board or committee of Christian education. In addition these steps assume that the teaching ministry of a congregation belongs to the entire congregation, and therefore the entire congregation needs to be kept abreast of the process and invited to participate.

1. Check to see if a mission statement currently exists. If so, review it to see if you need to develop a new one or simply revise the existing statement. If you do not have a mission statement or think the current one needs revision, follow the steps below.

2. Develop a list of people who should be involved in the development of the mission statement and at what points their involvement is key. Early on, teachers and students, both adult and youth, need to share their ideas. The church governing board needs to be kept abreast of the process throughout, to coordinate this statement with other mission statements and the overall mission statement of the church, and to give final affirmation. All members of the congregation

need to know what's taking place and should be invited to participate if they wish.

3. Spend time in prayer—listening and seeking to discern God's direction.

4. Study the Bible passages mentioned in chapter 2.

5. Make copies of Appendix B and ask interested members, teachers, and adult and youth students to complete and return it. Have board members complete it as well.

6. Collate the responses to Appendix B, noting where there is agreement and disagreement.

7. Begin drafting a mission statement based on the analyzed responses to Appendix B.

8. When you have a first draft, check it against your prayer and Bible study discoveries and any samples of other mission statements that you may have collected. Modify your statement as needed.

9. Duplicate your draft and invite members of the congregation to make comments.

10. Give attention to comments offered and develop a final draft of a mission statement to give to the governing body for consideration and affirmation.

11. Meanwhile, plan ways to communicate and use the statement, including in worship. Thank all persons who participated in the development of the mission statement.

Appendix B

Ten Purposes for a Christian Education Ministry

Read the following statements and then choose three that best state what you think is the overall aim of your church's Christian education ministry. Note that there is space to write in statements of your own. Be prepared to share your responses with others and to work toward a common understanding of your purpose.

____ to lead persons to follow Jesus Christ as Lord and Savior

____ to prepare persons to respond and witness to God's Word as revealed in Jesus Christ

____ to recruit new members for the church

____ to relate the message of the Bible to the life concerns of youth and adult students

____ to help persons understand and integrate into their lives the meanings and experiences of the Christian faith

____ to help persons discover the meaning of the gospel for their social, economic, spiritual, and political lives

____ to train persons to bring justice to the problems of the world

_____ to grow in understanding of what it means to be a
      Christian and a member of a church affiliated with
      a particular denomination

_____ to prepare people for ministry in the workplace, the
      community, the school, and the family

_____ to help people make the Christian faith meaningful in
      their lives, build and participate in the Christian
      community, and nurture Christian hope for them-
      selves and all other people

_____ Other

Mission Statement Checklist

Use this checklist to see how well your mission statement stands up against ten criteria. Place checks in the appropriate columns.

	Meets the Test	Falls Short	Not Sure
1. Helps us quickly and clearly express what we're about			
2. Is brief			
3. Avoids jargon			
4. Is believable			
5. Can be understood by someone not involved in writing it			
6. Is a good starting point for developing goals and objectives			
7. Can help us evaluate programs			
8. Can help us focus our resources of time, talent, and money			
9. Can help us determine priorities			
10. Can keep us on track			

Appendix D

Shaping a Vision for the Teaching Ministry of a Congregation

These steps assume that the initiating body for the shaping of a vision for the teaching ministry of a congregation is the board or committee of Christian education. These steps also assume that the entire congregation is responsible for a church's teaching ministry and therefore needs to be kept abreast of the process and invited to participate at appropriate points.

The process described below takes five to six hours to complete. It could be done at a weekend retreat or in three separate two-hour sessions. The core group of participants should be the board of Christian education supplemented with representatives from the larger congregation. Arrange for the participants to represent the diversity within the congregation— young and old, newcomers and old-timers, males and females, and so forth.

Session 1

1. Welcome participants and have them introduce themselves.

2. Describe the purpose and plan of all three sessions in general and this session in particular.

3. Divide into small groups of three or four persons each. Have persons share responses to each of the following open-ended statements: "What first interested me, and continues to excite me, about the teaching ministry of our congregation is . . ." and "What disappoints me about the teaching ministry of our congregation is . . ." Ask each group to be prepared to share these with the larger group.

4. Invite the small groups to share their responses to each of the open-ended statements. Do this quickly, recording on newsprint key words and phrases as appropriate under the headings "What Interests and Excites Us" and "What Disappoints Us."

5. Pause to give thanks to God for all the interesting and exciting things about the teaching ministry of your congregation and ask God's help in letting go of those things that disappoint and grieve people about the church's teaching ministry. Seek God's direction and guidance in shaping a vision for the teaching ministry of your congregation.

6. Indicate that next the group will explore some Scripture passages for clues on what might transform the church's teaching ministry and guide the church in a vision for the future. Participants will be looking for key words and phrases that suggest the ingredients of God's vision for the teaching ministry in the future. Divide into small groups and assign each group one of the following Scripture passages and questions. Ask the small groups to be prepared to share their findings with the entire group at the end of the session.

Group 1—Deuteronomy 6:4-9

What actions are commanded?
How might similar actions look if carried out today?

Group 2—Exodus 13:14-16

What teaching model is described in this brief account?
How might that model be employed in today's teaching?

Group 3—Matthew 28:18-20

By what authority are Christians commissioned to teach?

What promise is given to those who carry out this mandate?

Group 4—Ephesians 4:11-16

What does this passage imply about the relationship between teaching and other ministries of the church?

What purpose for teaching does the text commend?

Group 5—Luke 10:25-37

What are the key teaching methods that Jesus used?

What is his essential message?

How might Jesus' message and methods as shown in this passage be used today?

7. Invite the small groups to report. Note that the passages dealt with a variety of concerns related to the teaching ministry—actions, models, authority, relationship with other ministries, and message. For future use, record on newsprint key words and phrases under the heading "Biblical Insights."

8. Close the session with a benediction.

Session 2

(In preparation for this session, post the newsprint sheets from steps 4 and 7 of the previous session.)

1. Open the session with prayer.

2. Describe the plan for this session.

3. Share a few thoughts about the meaning of vision. Use ideas from chapter 2 of this book. Respond to questions and discuss the ideas as needed.

4. Have the group look at the "What Interests and Excites Us" and "What Disappoints Us" lists and note what is missing

or needs strengthening. Record these on newsprint under the heading "What's Missing and/or Needs Strengthening."

5. Indicate that in addition to what excites, what's missing and/or needs strengthening, and the insights from Scripture, the congregation needs to look at the current situation in which it finds itself. Invite the participants to identify teaching-ministry needs and concerns both within the congregation and within the community in which the church is located. Record these on newsprint under the heading "Situations and Needs Today" for all to see and for future reference. At this time, every idea needs to be recorded without debate.

6. Take a break at this point and arrange the following newsprint lists in front of the group: "What Interests and Excites Us," "What's Missing and/or Needs Strengthening," "Biblical Insights," and "Situation and Needs Today."

7. Following the break, ask each person to choose from the posted lists the five things he or she believes most need to be part of this particular church's vision for its teaching ministry. Before doing this, you may want to review what a vision is and is not. (See chapter 2.)

8. Tally the results. Pull from the list the five items with the most votes. Spend a few minutes looking at these and combining items as appropriate.

9. In closing, share words of thanksgiving to God about and for the group's work together.

Session 3

(In preparation for this session, post a newsprint sheet for each of the five items that most need to be part of the church's vision for its teaching ministry.)

1. Open with prayer.

2. Describe the plan for this session.

3. Review the five items that came out of the work of the previous session. Spend seven to eight minutes recording signs/actions/ideas for each of the five vision items. Remind

the group that every idea gets recorded and there is no debate. Set a timer if that would be helpful to keep the process moving. Indicate that this is to be a creative process in which the entire group is involved and that the lists will be worked on further in five small groups.

4. Divide participants into five small groups, and give each group a list. Ask each group to use the list to guide them in drafting a vision statement pertaining to their item. Remind participants of the characteristics of a vision statement by using information from chapter 2. Indicate that each of the five groups will actually be working on a component of a vision statement. Have the groups put their statements on newsprint for sharing with the total group later.

5. Ask the five groups to post their statements and report to the entire group.

6. After the groups have reported, indicate what will be done with the work of the group, thank people for participating, and offer a prayer of thanksgiving for the ideas and work of the group. You may want to develop a litany of thanksgiving using the five vision statements and a group refrain.

Note: The board or committee of Christian education will need to take the five vision statements and refine them into one statement of vision for the congregation's teaching ministry. When the board is finished, share the statement of vision with the church's governing body for consideration and affirmation and with the congregation for their information and support.

Appendix E

Taking Stock

A Self-Assessment Tool for Teachers

Take a few minutes to review the ten teaching tasks important to this time of charting a new course for the church's teaching ministry. Then reflect on how and when you carry out those tasks and/or others you may have added to the list. For each of the tasks, place a check in the appropriate column on the following page (A: I am effective, or B: I want to improve). Then go back over the list of tasks and choose one that you most want to work on. Star (*) that item and note in column C (Notes) a way you might work on that or a person who might help you. If you are completing this tool in a group, talk with one or two other persons when you've completed your self-assessment.

TASK	A I am effective	B I want to improve	C Notes
1. Being a companion on the journey with students			
2. Providing hospitality			
3. Giving attention to thresholds in people's lives			
4. Respecting all persons			
5. Granting freedom, yet making the boundaries clear			
6. Sharing and encouraging the biblical story and our stories			
7. Preparing people to be involved in the total life and mission of the congregation			
8. Reflecting with students on their experiences in the life and mission of the congregation			
9. Trying new ways of teaching			
10. Giving thanks			

Appendix F

Building a Leader Development Plan for Your Church: Some Steps to Take

The following steps are offered as one way to move ahead in planning for leadership development. Tailor the ideas to fit your situation. These steps assume that the initiating body for the shaping of a leader development plan for a congregation is the board or committee of Christian education. The plan can be developed to strengthen leadership within the local church and/or leadership for the community beyond the church.

1. Identify the major parts of your leader development plan, such as identifying potential leaders and teachers, training potential and current leaders and teachers, and supporting teachers and leaders in their personal faith development and in their ministries. Set these descriptions alongside your mission and vision statements. Then spend time in quiet reflection and prayer. Listen for what God is saying. Ask, "To what extent do the parts we have described here for our leader development plan fit our mission and vision?" When you are satisfied that you have a fit, move on to step #2.

2. State goals or objectives for each part of your plan. Determine what you want to accomplish or the results you want to see.

3. Throughout, as you work on developing your plan, seek input and involvement from current teachers and leaders and interested members of the congregation.

4. Then taking each major part, list possible strategies for each. Initially don't worry about whether or not they're feasible or cost-effective; that can come later. This is a time to be creative, so let the ideas flow without censoring any; build on one another's ideas and spin them into something more. Give yourselves permission to share even the wildest ideas.

5. Once you have a good list of possible strategies, step back from this work and let the ideas rest. Put them on the back burner, and see which ones come to the top. Look at them in light of the demographics of your congregation and ask if the strategies outlined are in tune with the membership of the congregation.

6. At a later time have individuals choose the two or three strategies in each of the plan's parts that would best accomplish the goals and/or objectives stated. After persons have shared their choices, see what directions are suggested. What ideas emerged as most important to most people? Can some be combined?

7. Decide as a group on two or three beginning or key strategies for each part of your leader development plan and assign a person or persons to each to begin work on implementing the strategies. If you have time, the group might spend some time in further developing or spelling out each of the strategies.

An Example of a Draft Outline of a Teacher Training Plan for Potential Teachers

I. Objectives and strategies

  A. to increase the core of interested, skilled, and committed people

    1. reinstate the use of an interest or gift finder

    2. offer a gifts identification workshop at least biennially

    3. share testimonies of current teachers in the newsletter or weekly order of worship

    4. be clear about what's required, but make it as easy as possible for people to avail themselves of training opportunities

    5. develop a covenant between teachers and the board of Christian education

  B. to equip inexperienced persons with skills, knowledge, and support

    1. invite interested persons to observe classes for a set period of time on Sunday mornings

    2. invite interested persons to be part of a yearlong Bible study group

    3. invite persons to regularly attend worship

    4. take a group of persons from the church to a regional Christian education training event and pay their way

    5. assign a mentor to each potential teacher

For Current Teachers

I. Objectives and strategies

  A. to retain skilled and committed people

    1. assign prayer and support partners to every teacher and class

2. schedule classes at a time that allows teachers to worship regularly

3. provide regular Bible study and faith development groups for teachers at times that are convenient for the majority of teachers

4. provide scholarships for people to attend regional teacher training events

5. have teachers complete a training-needs assessment form

B. to keep teachers on the cutting edge

1. offer advanced courses

2. offer courses responding to needs assessment of teachers

3. provide observers who will observe in a classroom at a teacher's request and give helpful feedback so that the teacher may grow in needed areas

4. hold training times on occasional Sunday mornings with provisions made for substitute teachers for those involved

Appendix G

Resources

Aleshire, Daniel O. *Faithcare: Ministering to All God's People through the Ages of Life.* Louisville: Westminster/John Knox, 1988. Provides thoughtful reading for the planners of family ministries and the congregation's total educational ministry.

Bass, Dorothy C., editor. *Practicing Our Faith: A Way of Life for a Searching People.* San Francisco: Jossey-Bass Publishers, 1997. Essays dealing with 12 time-honored practices shaped by the Christian community and important for today's church. Leader's guide available.

Blazier, Kenneth D., and Linda R. Isham, eds. *The Teaching Church at Work: A Manual for the Board of Christian Education, Revised Edition.* Valley Forge, Pa.: Judson Press, 1993. Give guidance for the chair and members of the board of Christian education, complete with workshop designs, charts, and assessment tools.

Boomershine, Thomas. *Story Journey: An Invitation to the Gospel as Storytelling.* Nashville: Abingdon Press, 1988. Offers a series of biblical stories to be learned and explored in a variety of ways; printed in episodes to facilitate memorization, with exegetical comments and suggestions about ways to connect the story with contemporary experience.

Chism, Keith A. *Christian Education for the African American Community: Teacher Training in the Black Church.*

Nashville: Discipleship Resources, 1995. Speaks to the importance of pastoral leadership, offers good biblical foundation, and has survey and evaluation tools in appendices.

Clapp, Steve. *Fifty Ways to Reach Young Singles, Couples and Families*. Ft. Wayne, In.: Christian Community, 6404 South Calhoun, 1995. To order, call 219-744-6510. Has an informative introduction followed by fifty practical ideas of things to try.

Crockett, Joseph. *Teaching Scripture from an African American Perspective*. Nashville: Discipleship Resources, 1990. Describes four distinct yet related teaching strategies: story, exile, sanctuary, and exodus.

Dvirnak, Ingrid, and Susan Gillies. *Renewing God's People: A Personal Prayer, Devotional and Study Guide*. Valley Forge, Pa.: National Ministries. To order, call 1-800-ABC-3-USA, ext. 2464. Includes a workplace-oriented guide to prayer, a two-week devotional guide, and study sessions. The design guide offers plans for a ministry of the laity in the workplace emphasis.

Foster, Charles R. *Educating Congregations: The Future of Christian Education*. Nashville: Abingdon Press, 1994. Offers an alternative vision of Christian education that is corporate and attentive to the whole of the congregation's life and helps people correlate the Bible and Christian tradition to their experience. The author uses a series of exercises to help readers reflect on their own congregational settings.

Foster, Charles R., and Theodore Brelsford. *We Are the Church Together: Cultural Diversity in Congregational Life*. Valley Forge, Pa.: Trinity Press International, 1996. Gives a well-documented, thorough, and serious look at the dynamics of multicultural churches, instructs about what helps, and cautions about the risks and costs.

Harris, Maria. *Fashion Me a People: Curriculum in the Church.* Louisville: Westminster/John Knox, 1989. Provides thoughtful reading for the planners of family ministries and the congregation's total educational ministry.

_____. *Proclaim Jubilee! A Spirituality for the Twenty-first Century.* Louisville: Westminster/John Knox, 1996. Explores the biblical jubilee as both a pattern of spirituality and model for religious education and ministry.

Jones, Idris W., revised by Ruth L. Spencer. *The Work of the Sunday School Superintendent.* Valley Forge, Pa.: Judson Press, 1994. Provides a clear guide for the responsibilities of the Sunday school superintendent and an overview of the program of the Sunday church school.

Mead, Loren B. *The Once and Future Church: Reinventing the Congregation for a New Mission Frontier.* Washington, D.C.: Alban Institute, 1991. Takes a broad look at past and present changes in the church and postulates a future to which those changes are calling us.

Moran, Gabriel. *Showing How: The Act of Teaching.* Harrisburg, Pa.: Trinity Press International, 1997. An important work on the meaning of teaching that explores the languages of teaching and draws out implications for education.

Nelson, C. Ellis, ed. *Congregations: Their Power to Form and Transform.* Louisville: Westminster/John Knox, 1988. Considers congregational transformation from a systemic point of view; includes essays from a variety of people including Carl Dudley, Mary Elizabeth Moore, Charles Foster, and Maria Harris.

Olsen, Charles M. *Transforming Church Boards into Communities of Spiritual Leaders.* Washington, D.C.: Alban Institute, 1995. Presents a bold vision of leadership and offers inspiring, practical ways the board can make its meetings become opportunities for deepening faith, developing leadership, and ultimately renewing the church.

Olson, Richard P., and Joe H. Leonard, Jr. *A New Day for Family Ministry.* Washington, D.C.: Alban Institute, 1996. Provides an important new look at family units today, how they are changing, and how congregations can adapt their life and ministry together to meet the needs and rhythms of today's families.

O'Neal, Debbie Trafton. *More than Glue and Glitter: A Classroom Guide for Volunteer Teachers.* Minneapolis: Augsburg Fortress, 1992. Gives suggestions for classroom organization, advice on planning lessons, storytelling ideas, music and worship suggestions, recipes for basic supplies, and much more—practical, down-to-earth advice for use in the classroom.

Osmer, Richard Robert. *Teaching for Faith: A Guide for Teachers of Adult Classes.* Louisville: Westminster/John Knox, 1992. Explores four dimensions of faith: faith as belief, as commitment, as relationship, and as mystery; describes different teaching approaches that can address each of these dimensions.

Pazmiño, Robert W. *By What Authority Do We Teach? Sources for Empowering Christian Educators.* Grand Rapids, Michigan: Baker Book House, 1994. Defines authority and how it is perceived and applies these factors to the ministry of Christian education. Completes a trilogy.

_____. *Foundational Issues in Christian Education: An Introduction in Evangelical Perspective, 2nd ed.* Grand Rapids, Michigan: Baker Book House, 1993. Encourages Christian educators to raise the foundational questions anew so we don't perpetuate antiquated conceptions and practices that are not faithful to the gospel. Part of a trilogy.

Russell, Keith A. *In Search of the Church: New Testament Images for Tomorrow's Congregations.* Washington, D.C.: Alban Institute, 1994. Describes a contemporary biblical study on images of the church in the New Testament with questions and exercises at the end of each chapter. Good for adult classes, leadership training, church retreats, and board or committee meetings.

Schuller, David S., ed. *Rethinking Christian Education: Explorations in Theory and Practice.* St. Louis: Chalice Press, 1993. Presents leading Christian educators' responses to the Search Institute study of effective Christian education in Protestant congregations by reflecting on the study's implications. It looks at the findings in light of ministry to children, youth, and adults as well as the role of the pastor as teacher and the role of seminaries in preparing leaders for the church's educational ministry.

Seymour, Jack L., ed. *Mapping Christian Education: Approaches to Congregational Learning.* Nashville: Abingdon Press, 1997. Well-known contributors deal with four themes: transformation, faith community, spiritual growth, and religious instruction.

Van Ness, Patricia W. *Transforming Bible Study with Children: A Guide for Learning Together.* Nashville: Abingdon Press, 1991. Shows how to present imaginative Bible study lessons that take advantage of the unique ways in which children learn; focuses on wonder, imagination, and prayer, rather than on information; demonstrates how to prepare a lesson so that this transformative process can take place.

White, James W. *Intergenerational Religious Education: Models, Theory, and Prescription for Interage Life and Learning in the Faith Community.* Birmingham, Ala.: Religious Education Press, 1988. Presents models of intergenerational religious education, examines relevant theories, offers curriculum and evaluation strategies, and explores a vision for the future of intergenerational religious education.

The Whole People of God (lectionary-based curriculum resources). Inver Grove Heights, Minn.: Logos Productions, Inc.

Wimberly, Anne Streaty. *Soul Stories: African American Christian Education.* Nashville: Abingdon Press, 1994. Describes a story method of teaching, relating it to African American heritage and grounding it in biblical understandings. While the book has been written with the African American church in mind, there is significant material on the story-linking process that is applicable to all types of racial/ethnic congregations.

Notes

Chapter 1: Looking for New Maps, While Working with Old Ones

1. Loren B. Mead, *The Once and Future Church: Reinventing the Congregation for a New Mission Frontier* (Washington, D.C.: Alban Institute, 1991), 73.

2. Patricia W. Van Ness, *Transforming Bible Study with Children: A Guide for Learning Together* (Nashville: Abingdon Press, 1991), 26.

3. Elizabeth Yates, *A Book of Hours* (Noroton, Conn.: Vineyard Books, Inc., 1976), 17.

4. *New Oxford Annotated Bible, New Revised Standard Version*, ed. Bruce M. Metzger and Roland E. Murphy (New York: Oxford University Press, 1991), 3 (OT).

Chapter 2: Seeing Our Destination More Clearly

1. George Barna, *The Power of Vision: How You Can Capture and Apply God's Vision for Your Ministry* (Ventura, Calif.: Regal Books, 1992), 28.

Chapter 3: Trying New Paths

1. This church uses *The Whole People of God*, a lectionary-based curriculum from Logos Productions, Inc.

2. John E. Fisk, "Integrating Worship and Sunday School" (Attleboro, Mass.).

3. Ibid.

4. Steve Jewett, "A Proposal Concerning Christian Education at Memorial Baptist Church" (Middlebury, Vt.).

Chapter 4: Teaching along the Way

1. Iris V. Cully and Kendig Brubaker Cully, eds., *Harper's Encyclopedia of Religious Education* (San Francisco: Harper & Row, Publishers, 1990), 532.

2. Ibid., 636.

3. See Charles R. Foster, "Communicating: Informal Conversation in the Congregation's Education," in *Congregations: Their Power to Form and Transform*, ed. C. Ellis Nelson (Atlanta: John Knox Press, 1988), and Maria Harris, *Fashion Me a People: Curriculum in the Church* (Louisville: Westminster/John Knox Press), 1989.

4. Three books by Judy Gattis Smith may be helpful for this task. They are listed in Appendix G, Resources.

5. Robert Ellsberg, ed. *Dorothy Day: Selected Writings* (Maryknoll, N.Y.: Orbis Books, 1992) in Jan L. Richardson, *Sacred Journeys: A Woman's Book of Daily Prayer* (Nashville: Upper Room Books, 1995), 320.

Related Titles Available from Judson Press

(1-800-458-3766)

Basic Teacher Skills: Handbook for Church School Teachers, Revised Edition, Richard E. Rusbuldt. Provides a solid foundation of skills needed to become an effective church school teacher.

Christian Education in the Small Church, Donald L. Griggs and Judy McKay Walther. Presents field-tested plans for achieving quality Christian education with limited resources.

40 Ways to Teach in Groups, Martha M. Leypoldt. Uses diagrams to teach forty distinct methods of teaching young people and adults.

Foundations for the Teaching Church, Grant W. Hanson. A teaching method that transcends the traditional classroom experience to encompass everything the church is and does.

Leading Small Groups: Basic Skills for Church and Community Organizations, Nathan W. Turner. Designed for those who want to be more effective small-group leaders in Christian education, church growth, evangelism, denominational workshops and conferences, college and seminary classes, and volunteer organizations.

Planning for Teaching Church School, Donald L. Griggs. Provides a guide for teachers who want to adapt a church school curriculum to their students' needs.

Student's Bible Atlas, Edited by H. H. Rowley. Twenty-six color maps and diagrams depict Ancient Near East, journey to the Promised Land, Palestine in the time of Christ, Paul's journeys, and the spread of Christianity. Index and glossary of cities and place names are keyed to maps and to biblical references.

The Teaching Church—Active in Mission, Paul D. and Katherine A. Gehris. The "how-to's" of mission education for today—its importance, the link between mission and evangelism, discipleship as a holistic way of life, and cooperative community ministries.

The Teaching Church at Work, Revised, Edited by Kenneth D. Blazier and Linda R. Isham. Designed to help the board of Christian education become more effective in planning and implementing in the local church a total teaching program modeled after the ministry of Jesus.

Work of the Sunday School Superintendent, Idris W. Jones; revised by Ruth L. Spencer. A helpful guide for outlining the Sunday church school superintendent's responsibility as both a spiritual leader and a Christian educator.